En Route To Destiny

Anticipating The Voyage To Destiny

> "In every person's weakness, there is a hidden strength."

Prisca Nambuusi

Copyright © 2015 by Prisca Nambuusi
All rights reserved

Unless otherwise stated, scriptures are taken from the
New King James Version of the Bible
Copyright © 1982 by Thomas Nelson, Inc. Used by permission All rights reserved.

All definitions unless otherwise indicated, are taken from
the Concise Oxford English Dictionary.

First published in 2015
This edition 2018

Published by Authentic Authors UK in 2015
www.authenticauthorsuk.com

Cover design by Samuel Alebioshu
Instagram: @wegrounded
Facebook: We Are Grounded

CONTENTS

Dedication v
Foreword vii
Endorsement ix
Introduction xi

Chapter One: The end from the beginning 2
The entry point of one's existence 3
The God of communication 5
God is a God of preparation 7
The human race 15

Chapter Two: Life, an open book theory test 19
What is a test? 20
The God of restoration 24
Rear view mirror 27
Your way or the highway 28
In every person's weakness, there is a hidden strength ... 28
Knowledge is NOT power 33

Chapter Three: Not everything is a quick-fix! 37
Practice does NOT make perfect 37
In every race, there is a pace 39

Chapter Four: Team destiny 43

Chapter Five: Esther's life-driven journey 48
Esther's windshield of faith 49
What is the difference between faith and belief? 50
Faith is not focusing on current circumstances 53

Conclusion 71
About the Author 74
Endnotes 75

DEDICATION

This book is dedicated to the reader who can relate to my story, which I will be sharing with you in a moment. Your struggles somehow aid you into becoming a stronger person than you might think. This book is just for you. Enjoy!

FOREWORD

Prisca Nambuusi's inspirational book 'En Route to Destiny' delivers fundamental principles that empower you to wheel yourself to a destination that will make you significant in your family, community, the nation as well as the world as a whole.

Her personal testimonies enable you to absorb strategies that will equip you to overcome hindrances on your way to destiny and in effect turning your weakness into strength, your pain into gain, your shame into fame, as well as any obstacle into a miracle.

It is a fascinating and practical approach to conquering the mind-set and behavioural patterns that can prevent you from fulfilling your destiny. I highly commend Prisca Nambuusi for this vital contribution to the world of faith, and also recommend to all.

Rev. Richard Appiah
(City Temple International Cultural
Centre Branch, Kumasi, Ghana).

ENDORSEMENT

THIS BOOK IS WELL ARTICULATED and a good read for anyone in faith as well as anyone who is struggling to realise that there is more to them than their situation. The author has challenged me and inspired me both where I am currently, and on my walk with God. This book has answered some of my inner questions as to why certain events took place in my life. The first chapter looks into the author's perspective on life and has left me wanting to know more about her. There's a need for preparation when it comes to destiny, and it is step by step to victory. Prisca has captured everything and everyone around her concerning destiny from an entirely new and different angle. The book has got me thinking that this is just how a book should be, and other readers will be able to define who they are when helping someone find their path. Well-done Prisca, I'm so proud of you!

~ Evangelist Dorcas Ghaniyat Akeem
(Blogger of God loves single moms)

INTRODUCTION

WHERE WOULD YOU LIKE TO be in 10 years from now? This question gets me every time. Why is it so difficult to answer? However, it is an important question relating to destiny. It may be difficult for some to answer this question because; we know at the back of our minds, that anything can happen, ten years from now. This line of thought ultimately puts us in the position to let life happen to us rather than for us. Hopefully, this will no longer be the case for you after you have read this book.

DISCONTENTMENT IS NOT YOUR FRIEND; EXCUSES ARE YOUR ENEMIES.

Some believers argue that our unproductive struggles are caused by lack of belief, but it is more than just that. Fear also has a part to play in our struggles. Statistics reveal that 92% of people never follow through on their new year's goals or they are consistent with achieving their goal until January 15th.[1] Why is this? Yes, they believe their goal is achievable. Yes they want it, but no they are afraid to let go of what they have, to make way for the new. Fear holds us back. Allowing fear is like leaving the door to your heart open to all kinds of ill thoughts and ideas.

As we dig deeper into God's word, we realise that there is more we can do beneath the surface of our struggles to make changes. We will soon realise that our struggles are a battle for survival and everything we need is within us. If we fail to plan effectively, it is very easy to blame outside influences for our shortcomings. In Mark 7:15-23, Jesus makes this bold statement. He was addressing multitudes and teaching about the traditions of men and the commandments of God.

[15] "There is nothing that enters a man from outside which can defile him; but the things which come out of him, those are the things that defile a man.... [18] "Are you thus without understanding also? Do you not perceive that whatever enters a man from outside cannot defile him, [19] because it does not enter his heart but his stomach... [20] What comes out of a man, that defiles a man. [21] For from within, out of the heart of men, proceed evil thoughts, adulteries, fornications, murders, [22] thefts, covetousness wickedness, deceit, lewdness, an evil eye, blasphemy, pride, foolishness. [23] All these evil things come from within and defile a man. (Mark 7:15-23)

The passage is speaking of the mindset of an individual. The heart houses our thoughts, and our actions reflect our thoughts. Therefore, we cannot blame outside influences but rather change our way of thinking and response to the world around us. Throughout the Bible, we are often told to 'repent' or 'renewal our mind' which means to change our thoughts or lifestyle.

Do not conform to the pattern of this world, but be transformed by the renewing of your mind... (Romans 12:2) (NIV)

Yes, the world has a pattern, and it's very easy to fall into that pattern. The patterns speak of our daily habits. We must be selective in the choices we make by having core values that fall in line with God's standards. We must also be selective with our choice of words when speaking to anyone. Words of self-defeat are just as harmful as speaking negatively to someone else. We must learn to speak positively on a daily basis, for a positive outcome.

Finding practical solutions to life struggles can be a challenge, but a challenge when embraced can lead to astounding results. This book aims to reach out to readers who struggle with the pressures of life and to share with you, what I have learned on the way to a successful breakthrough in 2014. No matter the barrier, whether financial, career or social barrier, I am confident that you will be encouraged and edified, just like many of my readers today.

MY STORY:

In 2014 I had experienced a series of short-term success and long periods of trials and setbacks, in my education, finance, and health. Nothing seemed to improve as I had hoped. From childhood, I was conditioned to believe that things happen for a reason and that I should 'hang on in there' when the going gets tough. Today I'm here to tell you that I have learned to never buy into the clichés and sayings of this world. Not to dismiss that nothing bad ever happens, but know that God will use your trials in life to grab your attention and bring you to your knees before Him. In earnest, prayer and not through stale prayers, by seeking Him, we turn from evil. In desperation for a breakthrough, I turned to study the word with diligence.

The Lord led me into a period of fasting. I call it the perfect accidental fast. I aimed to eat healthily so that I can be alert in my university assignments and exams, but only to find God in the process. Reading the Bible in times of desperation brought better results than I expected. I guess my mindset then, was determination and openness to the truth. I encourage you to read the scriptures for yourself, as will benefit your life considerably. One verse, in particular, stood out most, John 15:6-7 says,

If anyone does not abide in Me, he is cast out as a branch and is withered; and they gather them and throw them into the fire, and they are burned. ⁷If you abide in Me, and My words abide in you, you will ask what you desire, and it shall be done for you. (John 15:6-7)

I won't get into too much detail about the verse, but I know that the Lord is ever ready to provide His truth if we hunger for it. What most people forget or fail to realise is that the Lord resists the proud and gives grace to the humble. Meaning He hides the truth from those who are not willing to go deeper with Him, according to Matthew 13:11. These people are consumed with their career, wealth and everything the world has to offer, just like I was, at the time. The grace of God is truly a gift we cannot take lightly. The gift of Grace is similar to the gift of time. It is not tangible that we can wave it about and boast about it to others. Therefore, it is given to the humble. We need God's grace to apply the truth in our everyday walk. We are all accountable for our souls, and we must co-operate with the Lord to avoid falling into a deeper pit, totally contrary to the deepness He has called us to.

What is Destiny?

Destiny derives from the Latin word "destinare" meaning, to make firm or establish.[2] When you live your God-given life, you are aligned with God's plan for your life. You know that you are living your destined life when the results are joyful, delightful and fulfilling. Some people call this sheer luck or fate. We are to discover our purpose to live a life of fulfillment.

In order to enjoy the benefits of being a child of God; it is essential to accept Christ, who can do what no man can do for you. Put aside whatever bothers you and ask the Lord God in heaven to forgive you your sins, acknowledging that you are a sinner and believe in your heart that He has already washed your sins away. Confess with your mouth that Christ died on the cross to save you, and then rose from the dead to prove His sovereignty. Personally invite Christ into your life as the Lord of your soul and permit Him to transform you. Remember to thank Him for His unconditional love and grace in keeping you all this while.

Thank you, Jesus, for dying for me and giving me eternal life. Amen.

If you have made the step to pray as mentioned above, you are now on your way to a new refreshed way of life that fully depends on Christ the author and finisher of your destiny. Congratulations! This book is dedicated to you as a child of the living God.

LIFE IS AN OPEN BOOK THEORY TEST

Here, I equate human life to the build-up of a car and its main components. Find out how you can maintain and repair your destiny if it has been altered in any way. Find out how you can stay focused and be committed to your path of destiny to achieve positive outcomes.

Build a network of friends called 'Team Destiny.'

Think of your life as a race; you will know that a runner needs supporters. These are people who motivate, encourage and challenge you as you succeed to the next level. Having the right set of people around you is important. They are the support network for your progress. They push you and are willing to contribute towards your progress and add value to your life. Your support network does not necessarily have to know how to dream big, but they should have some understanding of the importance of your goals. The lame man in the Bible was among other lame people until he met Jesus, who challenged his situation. He had been in the same place far too long, yet in that same place, he arose by believing in a word spoken to him by Christ Jesus. In the fourth chapter, I briefly described what happens when the wrong set of people are in your life. At times, being around individuals who are in the same boat as you or who go through similar situations as you, may sometimes restrict you from thinking outside the box. Surround yourself with those who may see your situation from a different perspective, and perhaps help you in ways you would not expect.

Esther's life-driven journey

The final chapter describes a series of events that took place in Esther's race of life. The book of Esther is essential when it comes to the topic of destiny and purpose. This chapter I solely dedicated to the study of Esther's characteristics, not as to make her an ideal but to better understand the significance of her account in the Bible. What do we learn?

Final words

If God has confidence in us, then we ought to have faith in Him. I pray that the light of truth may guide you and that you may grow in strength, spiritually and emotionally. At some point in life, the plans of God for your life must be birthed out. Soon you will enjoy the fullness of joy that Jesus spoke of in John 15:11.

Chapter One

The end from the beginning

I WOKE UP EARLY ONE MORNING with the urge and desire to pray, thanking God for a new day, starting my day afresh. Immediately after praying, the Lord posed a confounding question. "Prisca, do you remember when you went to Sunday school as a young child?"

I replied. "Yes." He continued. "And do you remember how you didn't like Sunday school because you were embarrassed about always being the last one to find the Bible verses?" I said, "Yes Lord I remember it like it was yesterday." "Well, I know you didn't like it, but it was I all along. Your mother encouraged you to go because I was preparing you for where you are now headed."

I immediately burst into tears and sobbed like a baby. The Lord had more to say, but the tears just continued to stream down my face. I was amazed to have a real Father who is the King, who took care of me all those years back. I already knew Him as Our Heavenly Father, but not to that extent. Then I remembered a verse in Jeremiah 1.5. It reads,

"Before I formed you in the womb I knew you; before you were born I sanctified you; I ordained you a prophet to the nations." (Jeremiah 1:5)

The book of Jeremiah talks about God's instructions to Jeremiah to preach to the false priests and prophets of Israel, who caused God to anger, through disobedience and greed. In chapter one of Jeremiah God draws out a plan of what He wants to do with His people and that His people should take heed and follow His instructions. This verse is God's encouragement to Jeremiah and can also be ours.

THE ENTRY POINT OF ONE'S EXISTENCE

We were not created out of boredom. We were created out of love and simply because God is love. God created us and calls us His very own sons and daughters. To say "God does not exist" is like, giving birth to children who eventually grow up to believe that parents don't even exist, "there's no such thing as parents." Or "parents are not real." We did not appear from thin air, as most scientists like to describe the earth's existence, we arrived as babies from our parents and eventually grew (and still growing). Our human existence cannot by-pass the childbirth process. Any other way is considered strange for one to appear in thin air.

Nevertheless, God created us to exercise His love for us, through the childbirth of Christ Jesus. The world may reject God's proposal of love, but He has proven to be a God full of mercies, full of faith and full of His never-ending love. He wants to create a holy family and a holy nation. Abraham was obedient to God when he was told to sacrifice his son in Genesis 22. It showed that Abraham loved God more than anything and his son was an appreciation of God's love. This great sacrifice (which turned out to be a test), is also portrayed in the coming of the Son Jesus Christ, who was sacrificed for the world He loved so dear. It is a public display of love in action. This reminds me of the video footage I watched. One of the couples proposed to their beloved, in a public place full of people. It is a brave move to make, especially when the person proposing does not know how their loved one may react. The church is the bride of Christ and a time will come that all eyes will be on Christ *and* His beloved church, as mentioned in Revelation 21:2. The true bride of Christ (the church) will be revealed on the day of judgment when all eyes will be looking to the church for answers.

Let us change the existence scenario by asking a question. How do you know that God loves you? The answer to this question may require a lot of thought, and usually involves how we perceive love, especially from a young age. We develop our understanding of love by the social influence around us. God the Father gave us His word to teach us His love. Some people have a hard time believing that God truly cares for them. The question remains: How do you know that God loves you?

Proverbs 3:12 *tells us,*

For whom the Lord loves He corrects, just as a father the son in whom he delights.

The issue now is how well can we take God's instruction and follow His lead? He cares for us enough, so we don't fully rely on our own judgment. His ways are higher than ours, and His thoughts higher than our thoughts. He desires to make you prosperous. If you don't believe me, read the verse below for yourself.

'This book of the law shall not depart from your mouth; but thou shalt **meditate therein day and night,** that you mayest observe to do according to all that is written therein: for then you shalt **make thy way prosperous,** and then thou shalt have good success.' (Joshua 1:8)

To meditate means to reflect, ponder, ruminate, revolve constantly. According to the Hebrew translation,[3] when we meditate on God's word; we constantly fill our lives with His truth and wisdom, leading us to make the right decisions and to become successful. Meditating on God's words means, we are taking care of our inner man, so our inner man can grow. The older I became, the more I evolve along different paths of interests, emotionally, intellectually and spiritually. My point is that there is a need for growth in our Christian walk; mentally, spiritually and not just physically through acts of kindness.

THE GOD OF COMMUNICATION

The first stages of my breakthrough from struggles began by getting a deeper revelation of who God is and not just who people say He is. When you know God for yourself, no one can take that away from you! It sure is priceless.

Communication (not to be confused with conversation) is about the transformation of thoughts and words into meaningful actions that don't necessarily require a response. Let's put it this way, as you read this book. I am communicating vital information to you even though we are not both physically present together. Our tone or way of speaking may vary from person to person, depending on who we are speaking to. An example, when we email a professional company, we adjust our tone and choice of words in writing. It could be someone of authority whom we respect, such as a parental figure, a teacher and the like.

We may not see God physically, but through His word, we are assured that He is with us spiritually. In the past, I thought communication is about giving and receiving, but I have learned that how you receive information is just as important. It's similar to a T.V advertisement. They give you information, but you do not respond to the T.V directly. Instead, you respond by following their instruction. For example, they may ask you to "call the number on your screen now." They are simply inviting you to speak with a representative and use their service or make a purchase. Then they follow with a time frame, when and how you should contact them. God's word is somewhat like an ad; He communicates with us by inviting us to give Him a try. He did not ask us for money or food, but to heed to His instructions by faith (not in fear). When we respond to His call, we are letting Him know that we love Him. We acknowledge who He is through our actions and getting a better understanding of who we are through His love towards us. We find comfort and stability, in God, especially in difficult situations that have a purpose too.

Christ is our example to further better our relationship with God the Father. That was His purpose and plan from the beginning. The mistake we make as humans is to view God as separate being altogether. When meeting people for the first time, it is very easy to ask ourselves whether the other person 'ticks all the boxes. Do you have a list of boxes ticked for Christ to meet your human needs? It is worth noting what characteristics Jesus has and what role He plays in our life. Then we can look at what role the Holy Spirit and God the Father has in our lives so that we can have an effective prayer life.

Have you asked Him what His plans are for your life? If not, I encourage you to do so. Listen to His response. His response may come through a personal message or a dream, a situation or simply through His word. If you are lucky, His response may come directly from Him. Though we don't see Him, be diligent and demand a response from Him. He is a God of communication.

GOD IS A GOD OF PREPARATION

Many believe that the heavenly Father sits on His throne all day long watching tiny people moving around under His feet. The Bible warns us in Leviticus 26:1, that we should not make an image and likeness of Him.

You shall not make idols for yourselves; neither a carved image nor a sacred pillar shall you rear up for yourselves; nor shall you set up an engraved stone in your land, to bow to it; for I am the LORD your God. (Leviticus 26:1)

The verse does not suggest that we should not know Him. Our purpose in life is to know. Earlier in my Christian walk; I would think that idols and carved images were the same thing, just used interchangeably. However, an idol can also be an image or icon to represent God in a time of worship.[4] It is possible to idolize someone you have never met in person, having a false view of their success, without considering the background information to their success. It is all just an illusion. They often desire to follow in their footsteps with high expectations, not to be confused with the idea of having a role model who inevitably motivates or inspires you.

I loved God, but I didn't understand my purpose, yet we are called according to His purpose. Fair enough I didn't understand my purpose and *that* was the issue. The purpose was not my purpose but according to *His* purpose. His purpose was not for me to try and understand, but to trust that His purpose for me is good.

But as it is written: "Eye hath not seen, nor ear heard, neither have entered into the heart of man the things which God hath prepared for them that love Him."

Creating a mental image of God and what we think He is doing can bring about confusion. Confusion is a result of the retrospection against a counterfeit. The truth has been laid out for us in the Bible. No one can see God face-to-face and live. We *can,* however, get a glimpse of God's character through first-hand accounts of those who walked and talked with God in the Bible. At least this information is recorded for us, who believe in the true word of God.

What are the characteristics and traits of our heavenly Father? As we explore some of the natural characteristics of God in His divine nature and what He does, notice how they are all described in the present tense.

1. He thinks good thoughts towards us

How precious also are Your thoughts to me, O God! How great is the sum of them! [18] *if I should count them, they would be more in number than the sand; When I awake, I am still with You.* (Psalm 139:17-18.)

2. He brings streams out of the rock and opens rivers

I will open rivers in desolate heights, and fountains in the midst of the valley...[20] *That they may see and know, and consider and understand together, that the hand of the Lord has done this, and the holy one of Israel has created it* (Isaiah 41:18,20).

We know the lord has a hand and He creates anything with His hands.

3. He operates in authority (Elohim)

For the Lord of hosts has purposed, and who will annul it? His hand is stretched out, and who will turn it back?" (Isaiah 14:27)

4. He brings the new birth a child (El Elyon)

His business of creating new things did not end after seven days of creation. He continues to create people like you and me.

Genesis 1:1-3, Psalm 68, Mark 13:19).

5. He sees all things and knows all things (El Roi)

Psalm 139:7-12, Genesis 16:11).

6. He provides us with blessings. (El Shaddai or Yahweh/Yireh)

He is the sufficient source (Genesis 35:11, Psalm 90:2).

7. He is with us (Immanuel)

Isaiah 7:14, 8:8-10. Matthew 1:23).

8. He keeps His promises. (Jehovah)

He is the covenant keeper (Exodus 3:14, Psalm 102).

9. He heals (Jehovah Rapha)

Exodus 15:25-27, Psalm 103:3; Psalm 147:3, and 1 Peter 2:24).

10. He protects. (Jehovah-Rohi)

He is the shepherd (Psalm 23:1-3, Isaiah 53:6, Hebrews 13:20, Revelation 7:17).

11. He purifies.

He is righteous (Jehovah Tsidkenu)

(Jeremiah 23:5-6, 33:16, Ezekiel 36:26-27, 2 Corinthians 5:21)

12. He exists (Yahweh or YHWH)

He is the Lord (Exodus 3:14, Malachi 3:6).

13. He protects (Yahweh Nissi)

(Exodus 16:15)

14. He fathers (Abba)

The Lord fulfills His parental obligation, by providing, disciplining His people, and becoming a father to the fatherless, the widows and the orphans. As a Father, He will make sure that we not only survive but also succeed.

When my father and my mother forsake me, Then the Lord will take care of me. (Psalm 27:10)

The list is endless!

A person with a good character produces good works, not because good works produce good character.

A person once asked me, 'if the Queen of England is good?" It was such an open question that I had to consider it from different perspectives. "What is your interpretation of good?" I thought to myself. A verse came to mind:

Why do you call me good?" Jesus answered. "No one is good- except God alone. (Mark 10:18)

I could have easily ended there with the verse alone. Instead, I would like us to go deeper. Why then is being good so important, if only God is good?

2 Corinthians 10:12 says,

For we dare not class ourselves or compare ourselves with those, who commend themselves. But they, measuring themselves by themselves, and comparing themselves among themselves, are not wise. (2 Corinthians 10:12)

When Jesus said, "no one is good-except God alone." He was giving us a measuring tool by which we can model good behaviour. God is just and pure; is the perfect example when it comes to defining 'good.'

Another way to go about the question, "is the Queen good?" Is by asking, are those in authority good enough to go to heaven?' Firstly, God desires that no one person should perish. *Everyone* (Not just believers), who calls on the name of the Lord will be saved.

For this is the will of God, that by doing good you may put to silence the ignorance of foolish men. (1 Peter 2:15)

God's goodness involves sound wisdom. Some people don't want to know God because of His rules and commands. They don't wish to take wise counsel and see it as a restriction to their freedom, rather than a guide to reach their ultimate destiny. On the other hand, no one can be a Christian simply because their parents are Christians. Simply being a good Christian does not guarantee you a place in heaven, unless we execute the principles of our faith in the word of God. This can be said for another believers, who rely on the teachings of their denomination. Faith is not found in the wisdom of men but the wisdom of God. (1 Corinthians 2: 5). John Blanchard made a statement in his book; *can we be good without God?* He writes,

"Here is the amazing answer to the question, 'How can a righteous God ever wipe out anybody's sin and declare that person acceptable in His sight without bending the rules and compromising His righteousness?' To look at it from another angle, how can God punish sin (as He must) yet declare a sinner free from guilt and its consequences?" [5]

What a question! We thank God for the finished works of Jesus Christ on the cross.

Understand that God's love and strength work like a magnet.

Philippians 2:13 and 14 say, *for it is God who works in you both to will and do for His good pleasure…*[15] that you may become blameless and harmless, children of God without fault in the midst of a crooked and perverse generation… (Philippians 2:13,15)

It is easier to trust Jesus to take you to heaven than to try and go to heaven by your strength.

Without God, every wicked thing that could exist on earth would be found in us. In the book of Genesis chapter one, it tells us that the earth was void and dark. Darkness represents sin. The power of

God (the Holy Spirit) hovered over the waters of the earth; then God spoke light. In my view, the Light represents righteousness and truth, as Jesus is the light of the world the way and the truth. His purpose was to share the truth to mankind in the hope that they will believe in Him and not face the consequences of sin, which is the death.

'Energy cannot be created or destroyed; it can only be changed from one form to another' (Albert Einstein).[6]

I believe it is the same process that occurred when Jesus died on the cross. Our sins were transferred onto Christ to bear on our behalf. The debt that was left to us by Adam and Eve is sin and requires an advocate, the Lord Jesus Christ, who paid for our debt on the cross, once and for all. We have our own free will. Deuteronomy 30:15-20 lays out the options to choose life and good or death and evil. Choosing to let go of God and not wanting to associate yourself with Him, means we are choosing to carry the debt of sin by ourselves. Let that not be you. You would not want to miss out on the gift of grace and redemption.

Jonah 2: 8 reads,

"Those who regard worthless idols Forsake their own Mercy…

The purpose of being good is to put to silence the ignorance of foolish men.

As I mentioned before, being good comes with wisdom. Before Jesus ascended into heaven, He instructed the disciples to wait for the Helper (the Holy Spirit) to teach us, wise counsel. The Job description of the Holy Spirit of God, according to 1 Corinthians 2:10, is to reveal to us the hidden wisdom of God. Honestly, ask the Holy Spirit today to guide you into all truth and understanding. No one knows the things of God except the Spirit of God.

To summarise the purpose of your existence is to know the will of God, which is to do His good works, to silence the noise of foolish men who suppress the truth. How? Through the guidance, and wise counsel of the Holy Spirit; sent by Jesus. It is liberating to understand this fundamental truth. It is what keeps us followers of Christ going. It is the hope we have, in a world that cannot find hope. May the good Lord turn your complaints into opportunities that will activate the solutions to your problems. After all, God is the ultimate problem solver. He is the God of preparation.

Speaking from a place of frustration, rejection, and lack of motivation in 2013-14, I have learned that throughout the Bible and even today, God's plan is and has always been to restore humankind to Himself. He continues to restore us through His son Jesus.

Jesus came to reverse what took place in the Garden of Eden, and to win back, and gain our losses since the fall of man.

In Matthew 4:3, Jesus, who loves His church, was led to fast in the wilderness and was later tempted by satan, to turn stone to bread to eat. In the book of Genesis, Adam who loved his wife was tempted by the serpent (satan in disguise), to eat of the forbidden tree.

Jesus was tempted by the riches of the world while standing on a high desert top, in Matthew 4:8. Adam was tempted by the richness of the fruit of the forbidden tree. They lost the gift of eternal life, which Jesus came to restore, so we, have the privilege of eternal life. (Genesis 3:6)

Jesus was stripped and beaten when carrying the cross to Calvary (Mark 15:16-20) Adam and Eve were stripped, beaten by the enemy's trick and robbed of their right to dominate, leaving them to struggle in Genesis 3:24. Do you see the picture?

THE HUMAN RACE

I had the privilege of meeting a British Olympic athlete who was such an inspiration to the younger generation as she shared her journey and spoke about the hurdles she faced as she pursued her athletic career. She was a confident runner from a young age and faced challenges. She would explain how she dealt with those difficulties by focusing on her other gifts such as playing the guitar. Our gifts can often act as cushions to fall back on when things get tough. A runner can easily be tempted to give up the race, but what keeps him or her going is the key.

For our light affliction, which is but for a moment, is worketh for us a far more exceeding and eternal weight of glory. 2 (Corinthians 4:17)

Sometimes we give up on our hopes and dreams when we should be giving up on a lifestyle that does not contribute to our hopes and dreams. We are instructed to lay aside every weight of sin so that we can run the human race. It is clear that sin, which acts as a heavy load, can slow us down as we continue in our destiny. Have you ever tried running while carrying heavy baggage? It's certainly not easy and can cause some unnecessary delay in our progress.

In Numbers 14, we read of the Israelites in the wilderness. There journey to the promised land was delayed. It took them 40 years instead of Four years as God planned. What do you think delayed them? As they reached closer to the Promised Land, many of them gave up. They complained and wished they had returned to Egypt. Sometimes the most difficult situations in our lives is an indication of sudden change. The Israelites were familiar with the slave lifestyle they left behind in Egypt. Now, they needed to familiarise themselves with a new lifestyle in order to make it to the promise land. They were uncomfortable with being set free. They were still living in the Egypt mindset while entering a new land. In turn we can learn to change our mindset so we are prepared mentally by allowing God to transform us and make us capable of receiving His promises to us.

Just remember that when your hope runs out, the faithfulness of the Lord can get you back on track. This same backup plan worked for Jesus in the garden of Gethsemane

Saying, "Father, if it is your will, take this cup away from Me; nevertheless not My will, but Yours, be done. ^{43}Then an angel appeared to Him from heaven, strengthening Him. (Luke 22:42-43)

The same Spirit who raised Jesus from the dead can also raise you from all your troubles. Our weakness is His strength, and the victor's crown is awarded to you at the judgment seat of Christ because you have endured with the fortitude to enjoy eternal life in heaven.

REFLECTION/SUMMARY FOR CHAPTER ONE

- Are there common attributes about the people you communicate with?
- What is unique about the conversations you have?
- Do you have evidence of the positive results of your interactions?

- Know that you are born to serve a purpose.
- Your faith with the heavenly Father is unique and personal.
- Don't take God's grace for granted. Stay away from sin. Your stressful situations can be a blessing to strengthen and to build a bold but God-fearing life.

As evidenced by Adam's and Eve's situation, we require the following:

A PHYSICAL AND SPIRITUAL COVERING

He promises to clothe us with His glory and righteousness as He clothed Adam and his wife with the skin of tunics in Genesis 3:21. In the Garden of Eden, there was an end to Adam and Eve's riches and dominion. After they had eaten from the forbidden tree, they felt exposed. Their sin exposed them, and they ran for cover, desperately wanting to protect themselves from the presence of the Lord. They no longer felt safe and needed cover. They wanted to hide from the truth, which was God's word concerning the tree. Adam responded to God when asked why he ate of the tree: 'The woman whom You gave to be with me, she gave me of the tree, and ate' (Genesis 3:12).

PHYSICAL AND SPIRITUAL FOOD

To know God's character is to hear His voice and His language is to fill the void in our lives. My take on the situation here is that Adam took heed of Eve's voice rather than God's voice. Adam was responsible for communicating the instructions of God to Eve when she had arrived. Sin is as a result of separation from God, from God's gifts and from the purpose for which God has for us (see Romans 6:23). According to Adam and Eve, that feeling of guilt had to end at some point. Adam was hungry for God. He wailed at the churning of his yearning. He realised God is all he needed to fill the void in his heart. Adam had to work extra hard to till the ground. Naming the animals seemed easy for him initially, but now, he was struggling. The word of God is our spiritual food.

Chapter Two

Life is an open book theory test

Growing up in a Catholic church, people would tell me that my life is a test and that God was testing me. I did not quite understand which part of my life was a test, but it humbled me enough to make all attempts to have my name in God's good books by keeping all the Ten Commandments, (not to suggest that I was successful at it). The Bible makes one thing clear in Romans 3:20.

Therefore by the deeds of the law no flesh will be justified in His sight, for by the law is the knowledge of sin. (Romans 3:20)

What next? As I grew in faith, I understood that the Ten Commandments were given to us, not as a remedy for us to be right with God, but to point out our sins and acknowledge them as sins. Apostle Paul in the Bible puts it this way:

I would not have known sin except through the law. (Romans 7:7)

WHAT IS A TEST?

A test is an event or situation that reveals the strength or quality of someone or something. For example, a chair must carry a person's weight. A bridge must carry the load of many vehicles. They are tested for their strength when pressure is applied. A chair cannot carry the load of a truck. Why? Because, the chair was not designed for holding the truck. This is why God will never put on you more than you can bare. You are designed for a purpose that only you are capable of handling.

Do not conform to the pattern of this world, but be transformed by the renewing of your mind. **Then** *you will be able to test and approve what God's will is-his good pleasing and perfect will.* (Romans 12:2)

According to the verse, we just read, tests come when we have our minds renewed. Secondly, tests reveal God's perfect will, so that we don't fall into sin. Tests humble us and keep us at bay with God.

Esther in the Bible passed the test of faith. David had a slightly different approach to passing his test, yes he went through hurdles as a King to lead the nation, but God brought people like Nathan to guide him back into God's direction in 2 Samuel Chapter 12. It was a matter of obedience, though David was not perfect, he made it a priority always to be close to the Lord.

Job in the Bible was an upright man in God's eyes, yet he was tested at a particular point in his life. Why was this? We must understand that Job was wealthy, healthy and devoted to God. All was well until one day all was taken away from him. He had lost his assets, his ten sons, his health and his social life spiralled out of control. In Job 1:9-12, we read about the conversation that took place before the event of

Job's losses. The accuser of brethren (satan), goes before God and tells God, the only reason why Job is faithful, is because God had given him everything he could need and want in life and that if God took all that he had away from him, Job would curse God. In other words, satan tried to predict Job's reaction, and use that opportunity to distort Job's thoughts of God's love for him. The accuser, (satan) does not want you to be blessed and prosperous, and God commanded us in Joshua 1:8. If you remember the story of Adam and Eve, you'll find that Adam and Eve had everything until one day after eating from the forbidden tree they were struggling. They were ashamed and eventually hid from God. That union with God was broken; it was the plan of the enemy since the fall of man.

In Job's situation, God was raising a standard against the enemy. The accuser, who thought he knew all he could know about Job's relationship with God and to try and destroy it by destroying Job's integrity. The story of Job also reveals God's character of compassion and mercy, according to James 5:11.

Tests and trials can reveal the unshakable love and grace of God beyond human comprehension.

After all, that Job had gone through; this was his response:

Though he slay me, I will hope in him; (Job 13:15)

The book of Job is a lesson of inner-hope in the midst of trouble. We don't lean on the hope of others, but instead, find hope in God. People without hope often feel let down by society and therefore have a hard time trusting. They eventually become demotivated about their future and turn to suicidal attempts as their last resort. To put your hope in something is to put your trust in it. When we understand that our struggles are only temporary, we can understand how Job was able to put his hope and trust in God in the midst of a difficult period.

The story of Job ends so well when God gives Job much more than he ever had. Surely satan would have been furious by now, in trying to prove his point, that Job was only righteous because of God's provision in riches. Job's account ties in well with Romans 8:38-39.

For I am persuaded that neither death nor life, nor angels nor principalities nor powers, nor things to come, [39] nor height nor depth, nor any other created thing, shall be able to separate us from the love of God which is in Christ Jesus our Lord. (Romans 8:38-39)

Nothing can separate us from the love of God and love defeats evil.

During our times of testing, God seems to be far from us, and we learn to trust in Him and acknowledge Him above substances.

Let's take another look at the scene that took place in the Garden of Eden. Eve faced trial and questioning. She was questioned by the serpent (satan) about who she was, as in who she listens to and her relationship with God. Just like Job's account, the enemy was probably seeking to divide the relationship between God, Adam and Eve.

…*"Has God indeed said,* **'You shall not eat of every tree** *of the garden'?"* (Genesis 3:1)

Let's look at Genesis 2:16,17 for the original instruction God gave to Adam.

*And the LORD God commanded the man, saying, "Of **every tree of the garden you may freely eat;** ¹⁷ but of the tree of the knowledge of good and evil you shall not eat, for in the day that you eat of it you shall surely die."*

The Bible tells us that we should renew our mind daily so that repentance is not just a one-off occasion but a lifestyle of endurance. We repent by renewing our mind to escape the consequences that come with deceptions and snares of this world we live in today. We truly desire to change a pattern in our behaviour that acts as a stumbling block in our life. We cannot remove any heavy stumbling blocks ourselves but to seek Christ to overcome it, for His yoke is easy and His burden is light.

We tend to justify ourselves when in the wrong, but Christ came so that we may be justified of our sins through faith and believing in Him.

Repentance is the pathway to restoration, and the testing of faith is the pathway to endurance.

In many ways, life is like a car. The effort is required to maintain it. When looking to purchase a car, we look at the aim that the car will last and stand the test of time. A car cannot repair itself; rather it is the responsibility of the car owner to make conscious decisions to initiate the repairs. If a car has broken down and left on the roadside in disrepair, it is because proper care was not given, or simply the car is used to the max. When the car can be used no more, it is considered scrap. Other potential buyers may see the opportunity to restore the car to its former glory. As the bride of the Church of Christ, know that God does not waste His creation. He can repair aspects of your life when needed, binding the broken pieces with love, restoring you too to your full glory. Not worldly love, but the original, pure love of God.

A car also comes with a warranty – a guarantee that if anything were to go wrong, repairs could be readily made. I learned that I could not fix myself by myself, but the Manufacturer Himself, your Maker, and my Maker.

The speed bumps can represent the struggles we go through in life so that we can make careful decisions. They can be quite an obstacle for the driver who wishes to sail through in life. It is a part of our duty on the road of life, not to try and dodge them or do a U-turn but to go over them with care and receive victory on the other end. It's no good stopping at a speed bump and expecting it to move Romans 8:28, is a scripture I normally recited during the hard times.

And we know that all things work together for good to those who love God, to those who are the called according to His purpose. Romans 8:28

The speed may be slower as you reach the bumps, but the pace will pick up eventually. Life may seem slower or delayed at times. Remember to use those speed bump moments as an opportunity to pray for the Holy Spirit to strengthen you and quicken you.

THE GOD OF RESTORATION

While Jesus grew in stature, He was trained and brought up by His Jewish parents. Jesus lived on earth and understood the ways of man as well as the ways of His heavenly Father. He knew the direct pathway to God the Father and the way to life. He knew the path and the shortcut to life. He spoke saying "I am the way the truth and the life." To know the truth is one thing, to live the truth is another. We can avoid a labyrinth life if we make a conscious decision to follow Jesus' examples and guidance. He was skilled enough to operate the headlights of life, so others can see their way in life and plan a better future for themselves.

A car cannot change unless the initial owner decides to have it changed. Prayer does not move God but changes the person praying. God never changes and by allowing God to use us as the vessel to which we see His glory we are initially deciding for change called repentance. God is not engrossed by your sins but is willing just as you are to perfect you. He is the same yesterday, today and always. He is the God of restoration.

Oil

Oil is a substance that can bring wealth to a nation. It's amazing how many uses of oil there are. I will mention a few to illustrate how important oil is. The human body needs oil to keep the skin from drying. There are seasons in our life where our oil needs refreshing. When you open a bonnet of a car to check the oil and pull out the dip-stick, you'll find that the oil is a dark blackish colour if the oil has not been changed for a while. The oil should be a yellow golden colour to indicate that the oil is ok. When the oil is black, it is time to drain the oil filter. When life wares us down, we naturally feel empty inside, similar to the old oil drained from the oil filter of a vehicle. The feeling of emptiness is an uncomfortable one. This stage will be the best time to fill your inner man with the word of God, give extra time in prayer and fasting as prompted by the Holy Spirit. Practically apply the Word to your daily life.

Fuel

Buying fuel/gas for your tank is investing in the car. The fuel is harmful to us, but it is good for the vehicle. You are the engine, and the word of God is the fuel. Without fuel, the car cannot move. Our heart engine will require good investment by filling it with the appropriate resources. We need to invest in things that our heart engine can benefit from, so we don't find ourselves panicking, complaining and making noise to God like a broken down engine that needs servicing. What we feed our heart with is important if we want a healthy heart. Our spiritual heart acts the same way. We allow the necessary attributes that comply with the Manufacture's guide-the word. This means the words we speak and what we believe in matters.

When Eve was deceived at the tree of knowledge of evil, she allowed the deception of the serpent to fill her heart engine. Her destiny changed in a moment and was not able to function accordingly to God's standards. In reality, it is expensive to drain out the wrong fuel. Jesus' expense covers us, to drain out sin from our lives.

Water

Water is and always has been a source of physical survival. In Exodus 7:17 we read about the red sea turning to blood. It could have turned into something else, but I believe it was a demonstration of the water turning into wine during the Lord's Supper and the wedding at Cana in John 4:46 to represent His blood. Never the less the Egyptians could not use the water, and the same issue may have caused an economic downturn. It goes to show that God is indeed powerful and that all power belongs to Him.

The Holy Spirit symbolises the water, as mentioned in Genesis 1:1. Water is also the means to transport nutrients and remove waste products and toxins that the human body rejects, allowing the overall healthier cell life. (For source, see notes section) Without water there is dryness. Sometimes life can seem dry and empty or worse still it may seem flaky as though different aspects of life have fallen apart. To God be the glory, He can restore and bring you to life!

<u>Keys</u>

Jesus constantly spoke about the keys of the Kingdom. When we understand about keys on earth, we can understand the keys of the Kingdom. Keys are a symbol of authority and power. Do you know your rights as a child of the living God and the authority you have over the enemy? Adam and Eve had access to the Garden of Eden. Yes, there was security in the Garden of Eden, to prevent satan from entering, but somehow he used the Serpent to get in. In chapter one, I mentioned that the means to exist is through birth. The Serpent was a creature, but satan being a spirit used the serpent to gain access. The keys (power) of Adam and Eve eventually ended up in the wrong hands of Serpent and Adam and Eve were forbidden from entering Eden.

REAR VIEW MIRROR

Just like a rear view mirror of a car, we should focus less on our past and always keep our eyes on what is ahead of us. Notice how sin and unresolved issues tend to creep up from your past and not the future? We need to keep our behavior in check. Situations that are not dealt with early could rise to the surface later on in life. The small decisions we make could build their way up and have nowhere else to go but to the surface. Only acknowledge your past mistakes and move on. Only glance back at your past as a form of appreciation from where you came and keep moving forward.

Your way or the highway

The outcome of your destiny is determined by how well you are prepared when embarking on a journey. The mistake a lot of people make is not to plan their life but rather wait for life to happen to them. How important is this journey to you? Where do you need to be? If not, where can you get the resource to become successful in life? As dangerous as the world seems, we can, in turn, beautify our environment, because of the beautifying characteristic of God that we adopt from the beginning of creation. Jesus describes the Kingdom of God as His Father's house with many mansions. Just imagine having to navigate your way around many mansions. No wonder people sometimes get confused and lost in life! This is why we need instructions to lead us to our place of destiny and not to be lead by temptation, which leads to destruction.

In every person's weakness, there is a hidden strength

That strength remains hidden because we are conditioned as humans to make our struggles work against us rather than for us. We become comfortable with Living the status quo life.

When we look at the past behaviours of biblical figures, we learn that inside our weakness is a hidden strength in which we find solutions to life's difficulties. Moses was a stutterer, yet God called him to speak before the nations. He spoke to the nation despite his difficulties.

His strength was not in how well he spoke, but the importance of his message. Saul, who later became Paul, was a threat to the Christians, yet God had faith in him to carry the gospel of peace to the same Christians who were threatened by him.

God had prepared them so they could rely on God's strength rather than their strength or the strength of others. We are more familiar with our weaknesses that we overlook our ability in other areas.

When God created the earth, He saw how the earth was void, but He was not put off or discouraged, but rather willing to do something about it. What did He do?

Then God said, "Let there be light"; and there was light. And He saw the light was good, and God divided the light from the darkness.

God called the light Day and the darkness He called Night. So the evening and the morning were the first days. (Genesis 1:1-5)

God did not call the situation a disaster, but He simply created the opposite. He created light where it was dark and caused stability where there was void.

Sometimes the world works in opposites. To stand out, you may need to move in the opposite direction from everyone else. For example, sticking to the status quo until someone defines the odds. Very few people ever do anything about their current situation. It is dangerous to think that the void in your life has to remain. Acknowledging the need for change is the first step to a successful and fulfilled life. Our mindset has to change for the situation to change.

When God was making a change to the earth's appearance, He was thinking on a wider scale and made earth about humanity and not just about Adam. He made the earth with meticulous care, which tells us that the need to create the earth is a valuable one. He was so meticulous in His creation that the Bible even tells us the very strands of hair on a person's head can be counted. I can't think of any reason why anyone would want to count my hair strands. Surely this mind-blowing! God's nature in His creation is valuable and He ought to be valuable to us.

We must think big. Our God is a big God. Those who dream small only have enough to get by. Jesus is the Alpha and the Omega, (the first and last letter of the Greek alphabet). In English, that is the A-Z, roadmap, the way, the truth to everlasting Life.

God promised to prosper Jeremiah in verse 11 of Jeremiah chapter 29, but one thing for sure is that He did not state that the road would be easy.

Jeremiah was instructed by God to go to the potter's house. At the potter's house, he watched a demonstration of the skilled potter making vessels out of marred clay. Jeremiah was then instructed to speak to the men of Judah and tell them that they have two options. One is to turn from their evil ways and make their ways good, and then God would relent of the disaster that was ready for them.

The second option was to continue to do evil in the sight of God by ignoring the instructions of God's voice and have disaster come upon them. God is so passionate about speaking light into the void of your heart but requires your permission, your attention, and your patience. God will never force anything on anyone, so we are faced with choices every day.

You can choose to continue to call your disaster a disaster, but there is a better option. If you are reading this and you know you are facing, what seems like a disaster to you, use it as an opportunity to renew your passion for changing what seems almost impossible to change.

I reached a point in my life where things seemed stagnant. One thing depended on the other. I had thought that if one thing changes for the better, then eventually everything else would click into place. If you take a look at God's frustration, when the sins of the people multiplied, you would understand that the patterns of the world are a domino effect. Same goes for when we start our day. If we start the day prepared, it creates a domino effect of goodness.

THE BREAKTHROUGH POINT

I eventually gave up trying all that I had tried, after seeing that my health, my finances, and my education had little to no improvement. I had ran out of complaints, and I simply told the Lord, "This is your life that I am living, if this is how you want it, then so be it!" I had reached a dead end, and I had ran out of options.

It's no wonder 1 Corinthians 1:19 says this,

For it is written: "I will destroy the wisdom of the wise, and bring to nothing the understanding of the prudent." (1 Corinthians 1:19)

When I ran out of options, I ran out of God's wisdom (fuel). God used the blank page of my mind to map out a detour plan for me . What I initially depended on was no longer able to support me, at the time. I reached a point in my life where I no longer depended on the government, friends, and family but instead placed my full dependence on the giver of life. What took me a long time to do, I was then able to do in a short period, and I was able to make up for lost time. The results, yes the government stopped sending rent arrear notices, my exam grades improved and my health was back in shape, though I had shed a ton of weight due to stress and later due to fasting. People and strangers were charitable as they were concerned about my wellbeing. God can perfect all that concerns you, like Job, when he had more restored to him, just like Job in the Bible, who had more restored to him.

Friends, your pains and struggles are not a waste of time. God allows certain struggles to take place until we are done tolerating them, and until we give up coping on our own. If we can call upon the name of the Lord we can save time and resources.

So why can't God fix the problem?

The lack of readiness for a change is a problem. So what happened when disaster struck? They ran out of exits as I did. Know that what you call a disaster is, in fact, a platform for transformation. If you are in a difficult situation, ask the Lord to give you the courage to get through it safely and carefully. He promises in Psalm 91 that He is with us in the midst of trouble and that He will neither leave us nor forsake us. Our sins are unable to face the sovereignty of our God. Therefore, it was Jesus who truly knew what it felt like to be forsaken by God because He bore the sins and afflictions of humanity. Our definition of being forsaken is incomparable to Jesus' experience on the cross of Calvary.

KNOWLEDGE IS NOT POWER, BUT ACQUIRED KNOWLEDGE IS THE APPLICATION OF WISDOM.

In today's world, almost any piece of knowledge can easily pass as true, especially if the mainstream believes it. Eve happened to eat from the forbidden tree because she believed in a myth that she would be more like God. She was already made in the image and likeness of God but could not be more than God or above God. When we remove ourselves from under God's covering, we are automatically under the covering of sin. So we cannot be above God.

All power belongs to God who is full of knowledge. He is our source of light as we are instructed by Christ to be the light of the world. Picture this: a light bulb cannot light up without a balanced current or flow of power (electricity) circulating through it. The power to do more than you can ever imagine is according to the power in your prayer, giving no doubt. The Bible often spoke of giving us the power to trample over scorpions, the power to get wealth and so forth. This power does not come to us but operates through us so that we can make wise decisions.

Now to Him who is able to do exceedingly abundantly above all that we ask or think, according to the power that works in us,... (Ephesians 3:20)

Adam and Eve may have put their minds on the world market though their minds were not for sale. Jesus came to buy back that power so that you and I can reap the benefits of a truly meaningful life, with effective prayer life and a healthy relationship with our Father in heaven. Adam and Eve's action affected the next generation even today until we can believe that through Christ, the sins of our sinful nature, which was passed on spiritually, are now washed away.

BE TRANSFORMED BY THE RENEWAL OF YOUR MIND DAILY. RENEW THE PROSPERITY GUARANTEED BY READING THE WORD DAILY.

Let us look back to the scene in Matthew 21:13. Jesus was angry at the activity of buying and selling in the house of God. The house of God was meant to be a house of prayer, but people's minds were seeking to make gains and profits, which Jesus called, the den of thieves. This holds for us. The house of prayer is referring to us as the temple of God His dwelling place, filled with prayer. The congregation was robbed of their understanding of the word, which acts as the guarantee for success in life.

Your mind is not for sale! Each morning ask the Holy Spirit, the helper to give you the right knowledge to undergird your day and to equip you with the necessary tools, especially in these dark times.

May the word of God, which is sharper than a two-edged sword cut short any stumbling blocks and deceptions, to divide the lie from the truth concerning your life!

REFLECTIONS/SUMMARY OF CHAPTER TWO

You are the engine, and the word is the gas if you want to go somewhere in life! How has the finished work of Christ be able to transform you?

Living the word and acknowledging the word will acknowledge that authority has been given to you, to trample over evil thoughts.

A lie told a thousand times could pass a truth. Be diligent to remain on the Lord's true path.

All power belongs to God. He is our source of life and power supply to shine in the dark world. Don't try to be great by your strength! Depend on that power supply of knowledge to resolve anything.

Even Christ could not do any works without the Holy Spirit. The angels came to strengthen Him in the garden of Gethsemane.

Prayer does not move God but changes the person praying to make a positive impact on current situations.

Esther in the Bible kept the rhythm of prayer, she knew what fasting meant and executed it with faithfulness and commitment. She was desperate to see her Jewish people delivered and put her entire hope and trust in the power of God. She encouraged her team to step up and win the race together. It was a race against time and a race against failure. She was determined to outrun failure and by-pass her struggles. God made us winners and commanded us to prosper. What do you wish to achieve at the end of every month or every year? Does your faith please God? You would know in the innermost part of your being when God is pleased with you, and your actions fall in line with His word.

If He be in authority can command every living creature into being (to take form), He can command us to succeed.

There is a winning mechanism programmed in the power of your tongue. Your prayers are guaranteed to work gradually, if not instantly, just like a raising agent used in baking.

A person without the armour of God is like a car without a body or structure. Your life is structured, and your faith acts as the shield for your life. Your faith defends the truth about you against any lies. For example, there are times you may feel you're not good enough, put up the shield of faith and your vision for your life will be clearer. Your shield of faith is a reminder to you that you can do all things through Christ who is your source of strength.

Now we can see the importance of our cooperation with Christ when we pray. Amos3:3 says, can two work together, unless they are agreed

Chapter Three

Not everything is a quick-fix!

Practice does NOT make perfect

PRACTICE DOES NOT MAKE PERFECT, but it is the practice of patience that produces perfection. I'll give you a moment to think about that statement.

Firstly, we need to understand the meaning of the word 'practice'. Paul wrote that those who practice of such immoral behaviour would not enter the Kingdom of God. A practice of something is to repeat or make an activity habitual.

But let patience have its perfect work, that you may be perfect and complete, lacking nothing. (James 1:4).

I have learned that practicing patience is the act of trusting God through difficult times. In other words, we are not too quick to get out of trouble but can move forward out of trouble's way.

In many instances, we can be quick in our decisions, that we enter a situation, but cannot figure out how to get out of one. Picture yourself driving on a motorway, where there are plenty of exits, only one exit is more of convenience. Exits are usually accommodated by one or more service stations or a place to take a break. When we finally decide to exit safely, we can then feed our souls with the truth and be refreshed and sharp minded to go back on the journey of life. Our exits could be a period in which we dedicated time to draw closer to God. Jesus withdrew from the crowd numerous amounts of times. He chose to spend time with His heavenly Father until He was fully equipped again. He received visitations from angels to strengthen Him. The most astonishing part of the journey to life is not 'when' or 'where,' but rather, 'how' we make it to our destination.

Can one sue God for His delay in answering prayers? In writing this book, I learned that our sins do play a role in delaying our prayers. James 4;3 says,

When you ask, you do not receive, because you ask with wrong motives, that you may spend what you get on your pleasures. (NIV)

I learned that obedience is certainly better than sacrifice and that we should pray about the root of the matter rather than focus on the results. Your Father in heaven truly sees all you do and rewards you in ways you would not expect. Big commitments come with big rewards.

The Kingdom of God has a vision and a protocol. We read about the great commission in Mathew 28:16-20 and the vision of the New Jerusalem, are all part of God's plans.

And Jesus spoke and said to them, saying, "All authority has been given to Me in heaven and on earth. Go therefore and make disciples of all the nations, baptizing them in the name of the Father and of the Son and of the Holy Spirit, teaching them to observe all things that I have

commanded you; and lo, I am with you always, even to the end of the age." (Matthew 28:18-20)

IN EVERY RACE, THERE IS A PACE

When we look at God's plan and strategy for our lives, we can do much greater than what we, as individuals can ever imagine.

God has faith in you and is confident about you succeeding. That is why the race is not just for swift runners. The race is for the disciplined in mind, body and spirit. Your commitment to your success makes all the difference. Once the barriers are broken, and limitations fail, you have successfully gone beyond the thing you feared. The enemy does not want you to succeed or to be happy in life and would do all he can to bring you down. This is why Paul encourages us in James 1:2-4

"My brethren, count it all joy when you fall into various trials, knowing that the testing of your faith produces patience. But let patience have its perfect work, that you may be perfect and complete, lacking nothing." (James 1:2-4)

Your patience is the ability to trust God and not in man, to reach your success. Your faith is to believe in God's promises that they are true.

As we prepare for Jesus' coming, we are to practice and trust the principles of God's word in our day-to-day walk. We can learn from the past mistakes of others to prevent delays. The children of Israel who wandered in the wilderness for 40 years instead of four days, were groaning and were not patient enough, to trust the God of Moses for the promises that awaited them.

I was diagnosed with Adult Dyslexia in 2012. Those days were difficult. It was like living a new reality. One that was undesirable. Writing essays had not always been my strength, but I didn't consider it a big deal because I took pleasure in writing and learning. While studying a Postgraduate Degree in Building Surveying, I had to re-sit another year, to complete five modules. I had been deeply distressed at the time especially when the lack of financial provision added to the problem.

I quickly realised that the absence of financial provision was not the root of my problem. The Lord was just as fed up as I was.

With earnest prayer, God was able to shut certain doors in my life, and I began to speak positivity, as though I as taking my five-a-day verbally. I was especially praying against any source of my shortcomings, and the Lord began to open doors intellectually and financially, and I eventually passed all the modules with ease. Jesus is truly my help, though I didn't quite hold the Master's Degree I wanted, instead, I chose to rejoice with the Postgraduate degree, I celebrated the fact that it was not my strength but the Lord's, who provides beyond my wants and needs.

I believe our walk with God is about location as well as timing, where an individual can fully function in their allocated arena of life. A person who only moans will be his or her hindrance to moving forward in life. They have dwelled too long on the issues of current affairs just like the children of Israel in the wilderness. Dwelling in the positivity of your mind can help yield positivity.

Our brother Philippians 4:8 says,

Finally, brethren, whatever things are true, whatever things are noble, whatever things are just, whatever things are pure, whatever things are lovely, whatever things are of good report, if there is any virtue and if there is anything praiseworthy—meditate on these things. (Philippians 4:8)

Another version says "dwell on these things." To dwell is to live. Where is your mind located right now? Let your thoughts and intentions be pure by abiding in Christ.

People give up on their dreams simply because they have tolerated discouragement and given themselves excuses. A God-sized dream is usually difficult for someone else to fathom whereas people who dream small, will only have enough to get by. Neil Armstrong dreamt of travelling to the moon. I can imagine the sorts of comments he might have got. "You? To the moon? That's impossible." "You don't have what it takes for this job" and so forth, but he didn't give up. Being the first person to accomplish a safe landing on the moon meant that new legislation have to be made, which is an indication of broken barriers of limitation. People around him were committed to helping him accomplish his dream because he wouldn't have been able to do it all by himself. Neil Armstrong had the faith to go somewhere everyone else was afraid to go to the moon. For example Armstrong's faith is what kept him going despite how long it took.

We need faith to do the impossible. Ask the Lord to assist you with expanding your potential and maximising your time spent here on earth.

Reflection/Summary

- Practice does not make perfect but, it is the practice of patience that produces perfection. What you practice must be genuine so that perfection can take its place.
- Jesus was on earth for a limited time. He had a duty, and He was on assignment.
- God has faith in you and is confident about you succeeding. That's why the race is not just for swift runners.
- Which area of your life do you dedicate more of your time?
- What do you wish to achieve at the end of every month or every year?
- A God-sized dream is usually difficult for someone else to fathom.
- People who dream small will only have enough to get by.

Blessed is the man Who walks not in the counsel of the ungodly, Nor stands in the path of sinners, Nor sits in the seat of the scornful; (Psalm 1:1)

Chapter Four

Team Destiny

To reach your destiny, changes must take place. Sometimes a change does not have to be geographical; it can also be as simple as changing the way you view your workplace, home and other aspects of life.

When we think about the process of embarking a journey we think carefully about the following:

Where are you going? Who are you going with? How are you going? And so forth. It is much easier to plan for a journey when we know where we are going. If we can apply the same line of thought to our destinies, how much further can one go?

I don't think we can ever fully understand the overall master plan for our lives, but it can be revealed to us little by little. Knowing the full plans in one go can be too overwhelming, and the temptation for a self-willed driven purpose can turn us away from God and His blessings for us.

We are now confident to let go of what we've been holding on to as our support because God is the ultimate support. Should you entrust your destiny in the hands of someone who wants to see you fail? No way! So be sure you have the right set of a team around you. Instead of depending on others, others can depend on you for guidance; this is true discipleship.

WHAT YOU DO IN LIFE IS IMPORTANT, BUT WHO YOU ARE IS INEVITABLE.

A true disciple is not self-centred but takes an interest in another person's welfare. Their love for God is reflected in the relationship they have with one another. What you are committed to becomes part of your destiny and the Holy Spirit helps drive out the fear of commitment. What you do, says a lot about you than what you have. God knows how to bring the best in you, even in the difficult scenario.

Contributing to other people's lives and meeting the needs of others is what enhances a society. Esther contributed her prayer time and fasting on behalf of the Jews and the Jews did so likewise. The outcome was that God's people lived in harmony and feared of Him who saved them from their troubles rather than having fear of their situation.

Every individual needs an encourager, someone to cheer him or her on. These people are the support system.

Your destiny should not just be built on friendships but on faith. Friends come and go, but faith is steadfast in Christ. It is easy to be side-tracked from your true walk of success. Everyone has their lanes or paths constructed for them. Nothing should get in the way of your visions and dreams. What happens when there's no one to cheer you on? These are the times when you are urged to rely on God rather than everyone else fully. At moments like this, God brings the people to aid you in your kingdom assignment, when a major change is about to take place in your life. Yes, it's not easy to feel lonely, but in the quietness and stillness of your heart, you can hear the Holy Spirit. You are no longer distracted and attached to other people's visions but are now connected to your unique vision.

When you surround yourself with good people, ask yourself, does the other person's vision contribute to yours? What do you have in common? Ask the Lord to surround you with godly friends and family who will support and contribute to your goals and aspirations.

It is important that we put our faith in what God has spoken concerning our lives, regardless of what we may be going through. The Word of God was documented for your sake. Praises are to the Lord! If you feel that you've made a significant mistake in your life, know that the God who knows your heart has an escape route for you. Your job is to believe in Him as He makes a way where there seems to be no way. You will benefit from a community of like-minded people to help you remember God's love and concern for you.

When we make decisions without consulting God first, we may end up driven by other people's decisions. It is true that everyone needs advice. The right people will give you the right advice. Try asking someone how to get to Spain, when they have not been. What sort of answer would you expect to get back?

The one person we can be sure of that has been to heaven and to give us sound advice is Christ Jesus who ultimately spoke out and said, "It is finished!". He had finished His route through to live and is readily able to take us through the narrow route.

Do not walk in the path of the ungodly or stand in the counsel of sinners or sit in the seat of mockers. (Psalm 1:1)

We get to know people in different ways, directly or indirectly. e.g., we can get to know about the author through a book they write, their style, and their lifestyle, or through another person's feedback and through media. We can know a person by communicating with them directly, asking them questions, getting answers and finding out about them through the process.

Knowing God directly, through the Word of God, is God's message directly to you. It reveals His style, nature, and character. He gives life-changing facts about our lives. You can hear Him speak in the quiet moments and prayer. Indirectly He is known by another person's testimony and what God has done for them, through prophets, teachers, and evangelists.

We learn that He desires to have a relationship with us first before anyone else comes in. In most cases, we may depend on each other to grow together, and God uses different circumstances to mould us. Working through people is giving God access to perform miracles. Though we are not perfect, it does not stop Him from showing forth His glory no matter what.

REFLECTION/SUMMARY OF CHAPTER FOUR

- Who contributes to your heavenly assignment?
- Who or what has the greatest influence on your life; the government, the teachers or your friends?
- Ask the Lord to surround you with godly friends who will support and contribute to your goals and aspirations.

- Our Father in heaven wants a relationship with you first before anyone else.
- No one should discourage you, but uplift you and point you in God's direction. Knowing the character of Christ as our
- living example will help us discern what behaviour is of God and what behaviour is not of God.

The Bible encourages us to grow. *Be fruitful and multiply* (Genesis 1:28). For something or someone to multiply, they have to go through a process of change. Esther, along with other successful individuals, was God's vessel to carry His aspirations. Using the Word of God means we can defend ourselves against the harshness of today's world.

Don't wait to be an improved version of yourself but rather live in the present and be of great service to others. Do you respond or react to negative situations?

Chapter Five

Esther's life-driven journey

WHY TALK ABOUT ESTHER? MANY readers overlook the book of Esther in the Bible and often treat it as a storybook than a life lesson. We find that Esther succeeded in fulfilling her purpose by adhering to God's principles and as a result, her marriage became a blessing not only to herself and her relatives but also to the Jewish community and the entire nation.

"I will bless those who bless you, and whoever curses you I will curse; and all peoples on earth will be blessed through you." Genesis 12:3 (NIV)

In brief, the book of Esther speaks of a young Jewish lady adopted by her cousin, Mordecai, who was more like an uncle to her. Esther was chosen as a Queen fit for the king of Persia and leaves her home to take her position; then comes along Haman, the king's bearer, unaware of Queen Esther's Jewish background, eventually plots against the Jews. Haman demanded honor from Mordecai, being a Jew, refused to bow to him. This made Haman furious, and he deceived the king into issuing a decree for the mass murder of the Jews. Queen Esther learns of the news through Mordecai, her cousin and the community, and they go into a time of prayer and fasting before she approaches the king to address the matter. What will the king do now as the ruling cannot be reversed, other than to give the Jews the chance to fight back? The time came for the Jews to be killed by the neighbouring cities surrounding Persia and Persia itself. The Jews fought back and survived, just as God promised them in their cry for help.

If you were in Esther's shoes, how would you have handled the situation she faced? How can we apply Esther's tactics in our modern day-to-day lives and win back our lives? Esther, a young Jewish lady who trusted God for the success of the community, has demonstrated a series of characteristics worth studying. Although the book of Esther is a well-known book centered on the topic of destiny and purpose among believers, it is also a demonstration of God's love and sovereignty. No matter the situation we find ourselves in, we must learn to acknowledge God in the midst of that situation, especially when God seems silent.

ESTHER'S WINDSHIELD OF FAITH

When exploring the life of Esther, we find that she can find Biblical solutions without compromising the truth as a devoted Jew. Esther represented her future generation and was able to carry out God's ultimate plan.

The name Esther derives from the Hebrew word 'star.' What do stars do? Stars shine. Stars are only seen when it is dark and hide during the day. Esther remained hidden by not revealing her Jewish identity until it was time. Do you know that God can hide you until it is your appointed time to shine? Can you recall any moments in your life where this has already happened? At times, we may appear weak and invaluable to others, but this could be the time God chooses to hide you before you can be elevated to the next level. Sometimes the situation maybe dark and nothing may have improved and still God wants you to shine. This is the time to step out in faith and be bold. Stars are not shy that they cannot shine in the dark.

WHAT IS THE DIFFERENCE BETWEEN FAITH AND BELIEF?

You may be wondering by now what the difference is between faith and belief? Though faith and belief are close in meaning, they are still very different. Allow me to refresh your mind with this well-known verse among believers.

Now *faith is the substance of things hoped for, the evidence of things not seen.* (Hebrews 11:1)

This is such a short yet powerful verse. What is the verse saying? Let's break it down.

Firstly, the Hebrew word for faith is 'Pistis meaning, belief, persuasion, assurance, and firm conviction. The book of Hebrews goes on to list some examples of the faith of biblical figures and their outcome. I have listed a few for us to get a picture of what faith is.

Faith is not future but the now. (Hebrews 11:1)

We just read the previous verse. 'Now *faith*...' I like how the Bible is sometimes written in present tense. God communicates to us through His word continually.

Faith is to produce in us right living, right motives, and right thinking. (Hebrew 11:4)

Hebrews 11:4 gives us an example of what faith looks like through Abel who offered to give God a more excellent sacrifice than Cain. Not to suggest that Abel's offering was better, but rather the attitude in which he gave is key. Abel gave his best, knowing that God is His source of provision, not his labor. Cain, whose offering was rejected, is an example of what happens when we do not have faith. Cain began to show his true colours and his motives, displeased God. Instead of learning from Abel, he became very bitter.

Faith produces righteousness (Hebrews 11:7)

*By faith Noah, being divinely warned of **things not yet seen,** moved with godly fear, prepared an ark for the saving of household...*

Harbouring a godly fear will humble us and produce in us the righteousness of God. Noah feared the Lord to do what was required of him, which was to build the ark and warn people of the pending flood. It took years before Noah could see any rain or flood but trusted God in His plan. He did not doubt God's instruction.

Noah was rejected when he received a revelation that the earth was going to flood. He woke up every morning, built what he could of the Ark and rested by the evening. Then it was the same cycle for the next day and the next until he had finished building the ark. I can imagine people mocking him. Noah was a disciplined man; he also showed his ability to trust in God. His people could have easily deceived him, but he went along with God's big plan. I connote the church of Christ to an ark covered from the storms of life.

Faith is not wishful thinking that one should jump to their request. (Hebrews 11:11)

By faith, Sarah herself also received strength to conceive seed, and she bore a child when she was past the age because she judged Him faithful who had promised.

There is a need to build strength/power/energy in our faith; it does not come suddenly. In Sarah's case, she gained strength after a painful and cold experience of wanting a child in her old age; we read this in Genesis 21. This type of strength is developed in conjunction with patience and understanding. A person who has come out of a difficult situation develops strength, in the sense that he or she can make wiser decisions compared to their past, and not be easily persuaded to fall back into their old cycle.

Faith is reinforcing of Gods promises and pleases God.

But without faith, it is impossible to please Him, for he who comes to God must believe that He is and that He is a rewarder of those who diligently seek Him. (Hebrews 11.6)

The promises of God for your life can be found in Psalm 19:13. To be diligent is not to give up. The wait will soon be over. Hebrews 10:36 assures us of this.

Faith is not an idea separate from real life. (Hebrew 11:3)

By faith, we understand that the worlds were framed by the word of God so that the things which are seen were not made of things which are visible.

Faith is the opposite of fear (Hebrews 11:23)

By faith Moses, when he was born, was hidden three months by his parents, because they saw he was a beautiful child; and they were not afraid of the king's command.

We do not ignore or give into the problem but recognise the problem and presenting the problem to God and acknowledging God in the face of the problem, while trusting His direction even when you cannot hear from Him.

FAITH IS NOT FOCUSING ON CURRENT CIRCUMSTANCES

Remember, your circumstances are temporary, focus on your vision or goal, provided that it falls in line with God's will for your life. (Philippians 3:14)

Faith requires perseverance (Hebrews 11:26-27)

He regarded disgrace for the sake of Christ as of greater value than the treasures of Egypt, because he was looking ahead for his reward. By faith he left Egypt, not fearing the king's anger; **he persevered because he saw him who is invisible.**

There are a few keys we can pick up from this extract. Firstly, the verse is paraphrasing Exodus 2:11 and talks about Moses, who as a child, was put in a basket on the bank of the river Nile to escape the mass murder of all the newborn Hebrew boys in Egypt, because the Hebrew population had grown and outnumbered the Egyptians. The Egyptian king and his people were not happy about this. Moses was eventually found by Pharaoh's daughter and grew up in an Egyptian royal home. Moses was educated about his true identity as a Hebrew, as time went by, he was looking for a reward from God. Where did he look? He looked ahead, not behind him. Not in his past but ahead in hope. He had riches and everything that can make a human satisfied in life, yet he found the suffering of God's people to be more valuable than what he owned. Some of us regard material things as our reward. In Moses' case, the presence of God is esteemed more valuable as a reward that brings true lasting joy than the earthly treasure that brings only temporary joy.

<u>In summary, faith requires action.</u>

Based on James 2:17 I have listed a few actions of some of the biblical figures, who gained some results by having faith. When the Bible speaks of one who 'lacked faith,' to my understanding, it simply means they did not have the confidence/boldness to take action and walk in faith, even after hearing the truth. Do bear in mind that 'faith' and 'belief' are used interchangeably, and the definition varies from translation to translation, depending on the context of the passage. Now let's find out what belief is.

Belief: The Hebrew word is Pistueo, which means to trust, rely upon, commit to, confide in and have a mental persuasion.[8]

Belief in the Oxford dictionary is a strong feeling that something/somebody exists or is true; confidence that something or somebody is good or right.[9] In other words, a belief is the acceptance of an opinion or judgment in which a person is fully persuaded. These could be things that are not tangible such as a concept or an idea. Our belief can change over time as we gain more knowledge and understanding of something or someone.

However, accepting the word of God is not enough; we need to be able to trust in the Lord, that all His promises for our lives will surely come to pass in a matter of time. The Bible instructs us not to throw away our confidence.

Therefore do not cast away your confidence, which has great reward. For you have need of endurance, so that **after you have done the will of God,** *you may receive the promise:* (Hebrews 10:35-37)

Confidence speaks of the things we already know from experience, and know that they work. Think of how God has intervened for you in the past. What was the condition of your mindset back then? Do you believe He can do it again?

Still confused as to what faith is? Let's return to Hebrews 11:1; now *faith is the substance of things hoped for, the evidence of things not seen.* (Hebrews 11:1) King James Version (KJV).

Other translations use the words, reality, assurance, and conviction instead of 'substance.' From what we read in Hebrews with the list of examples, we understand that the word 'substance' mentioned in verse is the result or outcome of faith. Action must take place before the result can be evident. However when we read Hebrews 11:4, we are told that by faith Abel gave a more excellent offering than Cain.

Does this mean that Cain did not have faith to act in giving or did God have a preference? Surely Cain gave his offering too. Let's look at the chapter from the original verse in Genesis 4:3-7

And in the process of time it came to pass that Cain brought an offering of the fruit of the ground to the Lord, Abel also brought of the firstborn of his flock and their fat. And the Lord respected Abel and his offering, but He did not respect Cain and his offering. And Cain was very angry, and his countenance fell. So the Lord said to Cain, "Why are you angry?

And why has your countenance fallen? If you do well, will you not be accepted? And if you do not do well, sin lies at your door. And its desire is for you, but you should rule over it." Now Cain talked with Abel his brother; and it came to pass, when they were in the field, that Cain rose up against his brother and killed him. (Genesis 4:3-8)

Oh dear, Cain! On the bright side, there is some wisdom in God's response to Cain. "If you do well..." The answer to why most people struggle is right there before us.

Nevertheless, God was giving Cain another chance to do well, but he blew it by killing Abel, his brother. His attitude was all wrong. Also, I'd like to draw your attention to the part that says "You should rule over it." God was telling Cain that he should rule over sin, not sin to rule over him which is what was going on in this case. If you remember in the Garden of Eden, Adam was instructed by God to dominate (to rule) over the earth. We as believers can command sin to depart from us. Cain probably had too much competition with his brother, his wrong motives invited sin, leading to more sin. Did he think that God loved Abel more than him? The Bible doesn't say.

Some argue that God only required a blood sacrifice (hence why Abel's sacrifice was preferred) and that the offering of the firstborn sheep where blood sacrifice is required, would be a fore-shadow of Jesus (the lamb) crucified on the cross as an offering to God, for the atonement of our sins. On the contrary, when we read of blood sacrifices, usually they are accompanied by some sort of alter, which was not mentioned on this occasion.

Others say it is because the sheep was regarded more in value than the fruit. "More excellent" as described in Hebrews 11:4. Wouldn't you give anything worthless to a king or queen? God being sovereign deserves our best, but I digress.

How does this all relate to faith and destiny?

The point is that our faith must come with the right attitude, understanding and knowing what God requires of us and being filled with strength and diligence to do well.

In 1 John 3:12 we read that the works of Cain were evil.

Therefore his belief system was wrong, and he did the right things with the wrong motive. He didn't desire to make amends, and as a result, Cain struggled just like his father Adam, labouring at the sweat of his face in Genesis 3:19. Our belief system can influence our daily decisions, which leads to how we choose to react or respond to life. We can safely say that Cain's offering, in a way *did* matter, because it was the outcome of his faith and what he believed in. He could have copied Abel by bringing a sheep too, and his motive will still be wrong. When offering a gift to someone you love you would most likely give them your best. But if your attitude stinks more than the gift (real talk alert), it may be unfavourable to the receiver.

Now that we have an idea of what faith looks like and the consequences that come with not having faith, I would like to conclude this study on faith with one crucial verse.

But when you ask, you must believe and not doubt, because the one who doubts is like a wave of the sea, blown and tossed by the wind. ***That person should not expect to receive anything from the Lord.*** *Such a person is double-minded and unstable in all they do.* (James 1:6-8)

What are you expecting from the Lord? What doubts or limited beliefs might you have? What verse could counteract that limited belief? Is what you are expecting in line with your core values?

We can identify the moment our shield of faith goes down when we believe in the doubts of our mind and assume that our prayers are not working or the situation seems to be getting worse. We begin to buy into the lies that are used by the same tactics the enemy uses to deceive the world even till this day. The shield of faith must be up until the doubts in your life have been quenched. There is a complete sense of inner peace as a result of your prayer. Don't stop praying wait for the peace that Jesus promised.

Let's identify where the principles of faith and belief have been evident in the book of Esther.

Esther's humble beginning

Esther learned to keep her identity until the right time. She revealed her Jewish identity when an ungodly individual sought to destroy the Jews, and the Jews won the battle. My friend Jesus won the battle for you 2000 years ago on the cross. Claim it for yourself and your loved ones. Win every aspect of your life back through Christ Jesus. Don't fight your way, but take your concerns to the Lord. Remember to apply wisdom and defend yourself with the Law of God, as you would in a court case. Bring your case to the Lord who is Just and merciful.

Esther was submissive

She submitted to do what God required of her. To live on the knowledge and wisdom of the Lord, Esther was submissive to Mordecai her cousin knowing that they both served a great God, though they couldn't fully understand God's plan for their lives. In Esther 4:10 Mordecai told Hadassah (also known as Esther), not to give away her Jewish name. In order not to cause trouble, Esther didn't use her Hadassah name. Some of us have more than one name we like to be addressed by for whatever the reason may be. I believe it was similar to Esther's case. Esther 2:5-7 may hold the clue as to why Esther's uncle advised her not to use her real Jewish name. The social history, which stems back from sons of the tribe of Benjamin impacted Esther's generation, as she was a part of the family tree. The Jews from Jerusalem were made captive in the land of Babylon many years before Esther's birth. Hammedatha was among those who sought to have the Jews wiped out, during the reign of King Saul. God told King Saul to have the Amalekites destroyed as well as their possessions but left Agagite and Hammedatha. As a consequence, Hammedatha gave birth to Haman who became an archenemy to the Jews. God had prepared Esther, simply because of a mistake King Saul made generations back. Wow. Sometimes we wonder why we go through what we go through in our lives and ask ourselves 'why me?' Remember, you could be the solution to a long-standing problem, and only you can solve it according to God's will.

Understand that the stigma of being a Jew while living in the land of Shushan, Persia was evident, but it did not stop the plans of God from coming forth. God saves us and prepares us for greater. For someone to save something is an indication that they are reserving or separating something or someone for future use. Esther separated herself during the time of worship. She showed her appreciation by adopting a lifestyle of worship and adoration to the heavenly Father, before and after the 12 months of preparation to replace former queen Vashti.

Esther was determined

Esther may have been far from a luxurious living to start with, but she remained diligent and faithful and was determined to find a biblical solution for the Jews who were under threat. Esther was able to initiate a three-day fast. As a result, She was given the ability to make difficult decisions in the face of opposition and was willing to sacrifice her efforts. It is dangerous to believe that we don't need God in the matter. God knows our hearts, but we are to act in faith and not in fear.

There are different reasons to fast, fasting to intercede, fasting for a miracle or desire to know God's will. But in Esther's case, it was the need for freedom from bondage. David in the Bible declared a fast, but the Lord did not approve of their fast, why? Find out why this was in 2 Samuel 16:20-19:8. This goes to show that God takes our act of fasting seriously and again it can only be done properly by asking for God's mercies and strength. How does this relate to your destiny? Remember Cain whose offering was rejected by God. God punishes sin, but because He is merciful, He provides a way for us to be in right standing, despite our failings. He did this by taking the punishment upon Himself. We believe and accept that Christ not only covers our wrong doings but transforms us and fasting prepares our hearts for Him to do so.

When praying, I like to picture myself wearing the full armour of God, as described in Ephesians 6:16. Similar to the Jewish community who were under attack by the wicked, we can fight against the attack of our faith in Christ. The doubts are the arrow and the shield is your faith. Shield yourself from any physical distractions and thoughts that will slow down the momentum of your prayer. The momentum is what helps build your faith. Your earnest prayer to God is more powerful than you think and the enemy will always seek to terminate it, which is why people struggle to pray.

Above all taking the shield of faith with which you may be able to quench all the fiery darts of the wicked one and take the helmet of salvation, and the sword of the spirit, which is the word of God; praying always with all prayer and supplication for all the saints... (Ephesians 6:16)

ESTHER REMAINED HUMBLE IN LEADERSHIP

She was loyal to those whom God brought into her life. She developed the characteristics of a servant's heart even in the midst of trouble.

In Esther 1:8 the King showed poor leadership skills by implementing a law that allowed his household to do according to their own pleasure. They were allowed to drink as much alcohol as desired. This could lead to addiction and waywardness. 1 Corinthians 6:10 warns us of the consequence of excessive drinking.

nor thieves, nor covetous, nor drunkards, nor revilers, nor extortioners will inherit the kingdom of God. (1 Corinthians 6:10)

Instead, we are instructed to...

Be sober, be vigilant; because your adversary the devil, as a roaring lion, walketh about, seeking whom he may devour: (1 Peter 5:8)

Esther, on the other hand, portrayed good leadership skills by being resourceful, imaginative and putting her skills to the best use. Her skills and gifts were given to her by God's word from birth. She discovered her skills and utilised them over time. She was reliable and was trusted by God to use the gifts given to her. She was decisive in her decisions by basing them on God's perfect will.

She was open to others ideas and instructions and was challenged to change her circumstance for the better. When she prayed, her environment changed. Esther respected those in authority but as brothers and sisters in the Lord, no matter their personality or their position. Her life was in order, and she was an accomplishment of God's manifestation when allowing God to order her steps.

ESTHER WAS FAITHFUL

Esther took a giant step of faith to see the King. She could have been anybody but the King recognised her, and he held up the sceptre, even though she did not have the King's approval to enter his court.

On Judgment day it is our robe of righteousness that we are identified as true sons and daughters of the righteous King, recognised by the father, having followed His precepts and instructions. Either that or satan's identification number (SIN)

Matthew 7:21-23 says,

"Not everyone who says to Me, 'Lord, Lord,' shall enter the kingdom of heaven, but he who does the will of My Father in heaven. 22 Many will say to Me in that day, 'Lord, Lord, have we not prophesied in Your name, cast out demons in Your name, and done many wonders in Your name?' 23 And then I will declare to them, 'I never knew you; depart from Me, you who practice lawlessness!'

Psalm 45 says,

Your throne, O God, is forever and ever; A sceptre of righteousness is the sceptre of Your kingdom.

The earth is His footstool, heaven is His throne, and God's elect is His sceptre. We are the righteousness of God, called for His purposes and life and death are in the power of our tongue. We are the voice to speak life and encourage others but to defeat sin. Now we are to come in the presence of God with boldness and as a true child of God through the bloodshed of Jesus the Christ.

Esther appeared to the King, and the King saved her life by lifting the sceptre, because Esther was the King's bride. The Bible tells us that no one can see the King and live, similar to the protected court in which Esther entered into, without an invitation from the king. Glory be to Jesus in whom we the church are His bride, has made a way that we can connect to God. So come to God with boldness and sincerity. Be faithful to Gods plans to guide you in life. Speak to God often in every decision you make. The promises of God are yes and Amen. Don't let the enemy bully you out of God's presence! God loves you and cares for you.

EXPOSING THE HAMAN IN YOUR LIFE

Allow me to draw your attention to Joshua 24:6-9. Here we read of a similar situation to Queen Esther and Persia.

God was making a covenant to the tribes of Isreal, at the same time testing their faithfulness to worship Him and no other gods, as Joshua leads them into Shechem to get to Canaan, the Promised Land.

⁸ And I brought you into the land of the Amorites, who dwelt on the other side of the Jordan, **and they fought with you. But I gave them into your hand, that you might possess their land**, *and I destroyed them from before you. ⁹ Then Balak the son of Zippor, king of Moab, arose to make war against Israel, and sent and called Balaam the son of Beor to curse you. ¹⁰ But I would not listen to Balaam; therefore he continued to bless you. So I delivered you out of his hand*

Joshua's account gives us a better understanding as to how God operates and the need for us to co-operate with Him. Similar to the Jews fighting back in the book of Esther, the tribes of Israel fought the enemies in pitch black darkness, to which God says, *"I gave them into your hand, that you might possess their land."* The tribes of Israel though were rebellious previously, changed their ways to serve the Lord wholeheartedly, only because they had witnessed the mighty works of God's hands for their salvation. We cannot blame every bad situation on the enemy.

How does Joshua's story relate to the book of Esther? Haman was an archenemy used by God, so the outcome would be that the Jews lived in Persia in peace. Ecclesiastes 5:10 tells us that a person who depends on their riches is never 100% satisfied with themselves. Haman was not happy because of Mordecai, who refused to bow to him. This bothered him to the point that nothing else really mattered to him than to see Mordecai killed. What does it profit a man if he gains the whole world? The true joy of the Lord is the strength of our hearts.

Haman sought the diviners and sorcerers to work out the best day to have the Jews destroyed. They cast their lots, similar to flipping a coin to see if it will land on heads or tails. The results fell on the 11th month, which gave the Jews almost a year's notice to get ready for battle. That's a whole year that Haman was willing to wait in order to kill the Jews. In God's eyes, it would be enough time for the Jews to recover from the shock of the bad news they were about to receive! The Bible says in Proverbs 16:33 that every decision is controlled by God. We as Christians are to seek God in our decision-making and not through secular means.

In Esther chapter three, Haman deceived the King to get the Jews destroyed through a written decree. When a decree is made, it cannot be changed. Little did King Ahasureus know, that he was signing up to have his wife killed! We as Christians we are reminded that we are sealed by the Holy Spirit and nothing by any means should hurt us. It is the Lord's signature stamp when we obey Him that is!

The City of Shushan was in a panic state, and it had not occurred to Esther at that point. Just know that God is with us in the midst of trouble as He promised in Psalm 91. Learn to acknowledge Him. God is bigger than any problem and allows certain situations to take place so we can hold on to Him. This week thank God in prayer for all His benefits.

UP TO HALF OF MY KINGDOM

In Esther 7:1-8 Kings were only allowed to own up to 50% of the Kingdom so that they wouldn't make crazy promises just anyhow. Esther chose that particular moment to expose Haman's plot and to reveal her Jewish identity.

Our sister Proverbs 26:27 says,

Whoever digs a pit will fall into it, And he who rolls a stone will have it roll back on him (Proverbs 26:27)

In Esther 7:8 Haman became panic-stricken and later violates the palace orders by getting too close to the Queen, whilst he fell across the couch. (I imagine this was his instant reaction.) When we realise our wrongdoing, it is important not to act in fear by making rash decisions to try and cover up the mistake. The blood of Jesus has the power to cover your mistakes whether hidden or exposed. Adam and Eve tried to cover-up their mistake when they realised their shame could not stand in the omnipotence and dwelling place of God, so they were sent out of the Garden.

His glory acts like a magnet that when we do the opposite of what God tells us, we automatically do not experience open heaven and feel that God is far from us. God is always there to reconcile with you. The blood of Christ removes any hindrances, so you come back to your rightful place as a true son and daughter of the living God.

Haman was hanged on the gallows, which he created against the Jews. "Ouch!" It is in situations like this that God's sovereignty alone is enough to destroy His enemies. The presence of God alone can destroy yokes. Haman was gone, but the decree, which couldn't change, was still there. The decree was the law that made Genocide legal at that time. Remember the decree had gone out even to the remaining 26 provinces that King Xeres reigned over, so the other Jews in various places of the earth were also affected.

PEER PRESSURE

Remember it was not Haman's idea to build the gallows for Mordecai but the advice of his wife, in Esther 5:14. The gallows were 50 cubits, which is 22.9 m high. (The New Living Translation, suggests 75 feet) My, oh my! It would be equivalent to five standard double-decker buses stacked on top of each other. Haman's family were probably fed up of seeing their Haman so unhappy and thought that by getting rid of Mordecai that they would be getting rid of the problem.

As children of God, we rely on God even in the face of our enemies. Perhaps someone has mistreated you. The Bible says; He that touches God's people touches the apple of God's eye. In other words, God Himself can feel your pains and hurt since He dwells in us. As children of God, we should not be afraid of men and let God be God.

We must remain content with holiness and to mimic the true nature of God. We cannot do it alone. Every day we become more and more like Christ. Thank goodness for the blood of Jesus. A penalty we deserved, He stepped in and paid for us, that whoever believes in Him will be saved from darkness and the hidden plots of man. Knowing the truth is what would set us free.

Surround yourself with godly people and ask yourself, who in your circle of friends contributes to your Kingdom assignment?

ESTHER ENDURED

Though the battle seemed to take a long time, the battle was not hers but the Lord's. Having the gift of endurance is the power tool to accomplish God's will.

And let us not grow weary while doing good, for in due season we shall reap if we do not lose heart. (Galatians 6:9)

Let's look at Joshua 24:1-6 And Joshua gathered all the tribes of Israel to Shechem, and called for the elders of Israel, and for their heads, and for their judges, and for their officers; and they presented themselves before God.

² And Joshua said unto all the people, Thus saith the LORD God of Israel, Your fathers dwelt on the other side of the flood in old time, even Terah, the father of Abraham, and the father of Nachor: and they served other gods.

³ And I took your father Abraham from the other side of the flood, and led him throughout all the land of Canaan, and multiplied his seed, and gave him Isaac.

⁴ And I gave unto Isaac Jacob and Esau: and I gave unto Esau mount Seir, to possess it; but Jacob and his children went down into Egypt.

⁵ I sent Moses also and Aaron, and I plagued Egypt, according to that which I did among them: and afterward I brought you out.

⁶ And I brought your fathers out of Egypt: and ye came unto the sea; and the Egyptians pursued after your fathers with chariots and horsemen unto the Red sea.

Let us pray; I declare in the name of Jesus that from today as you present yourself before God, you will be brought out of every trouble in your life. You will not serve other gods rather the God of Isaac. Your seeds will be multiple. Amen.

SUMMARY

The plans of God for your life are enormous, and not everyone is capable of handling an enormous task at the stage they may be at, but God trusts you enough to reveal His dreams for your life. King Xeres trusted Haman at first but loved Esther and was faithful to household principles, which meant that he could not spare Haman because he was a threat undercover, he was the baby in the back seat of the vehicle to carry God's ultimate plan.

Be mindful of your motives. Do your motives please God, you or people? It is very easy today to buy into lies without realising, constantly checking in with God's word and make sure that your actions are in line with the word. Thank goodness for our conscience that when the Holy Spirit convicts us, it is up to us to correct our decisions, for God is the ultimate judge to reign in us.

What if Esther chose to give up? But she didn't because she kept God's command. She often withdrew herself to worship God and to fast for the nation.

Because you have kept My command to persevere, I also will keep you from the hour of trial which shall come upon the whole world, to test those who dwell on the earth. (Revelation 3:10)

Don't compromise who you are, stand out.

Take your concerns to the Lord, Come to God with boldness and sincerity. Ask the Lord to show you how to pray earnestly.

The conviction of sin is only God's mercy extended to you. Don't let the enemy bully you out of God's presence.

I came across a famous quote by Eugene V. Debs.

"It is better to vote for what you want and not get it than to vote for what you don't want and get it. (See Endnotes for source).

Kings and Queens approve of an idea before it takes place. We are called to royal priesthood according to heavenly principles we are to learn to abide by it for all-round blessings and benefits of the Kingdom. When we say yes or no we are either allow or disapprove certain aspects in our lives. Keep on praying and demand results. Put pressure on the Word of God and not on man. Vengeance belongs to the Lord, according to Romans 12:19. Put pressure on the word before the world puts pressure on you. For example, we can include verses in our prayer like this:

May the Lord continually enrich you to grow in the Love and the full knowledge of Christ. May this remaining year be filled with light to see God's plan unravel. I come against confusion and doubt, and I declare sound mind, peace, and righteousness in Jesus' name. Amen.

CONCLUSION

My last question to you is, how will you know that you have reached your destiny? I'm answering this question based on my experience and growth. The rate of growth depends on how well I can digest the word of God, understand the word and put it to practice. To pursue my destiny also depends on how hungry I am to discover my purpose on earth.

I discovered that the more I sought God about my purpose, the more I gained divine revelation from Him. In primary school I won book competitions, became a librarian as well as a prefect and made it on the front cover of a newspaper for best-dressed book character, during world book day. Mind you, I only joined these activities to build my confidence, not knowing that a time will come that I would write books for people to read. Why am I sharing this with you? As a believer we wonder what our purpose is without realizing that we have been walking in our purpose from birth. The things we take interest in and the skills we develop are all key to our purpose. God allows circumstances and situations to appear in our lives so we can be well developed in our character, in order to keep a good integrity that reflects God's glory. Allow Him to develop you. As He develops you, He reveals your flaws, not to shame you, but because the enemy will use your flaws against you to persecute you. Once you are self-aware and recognise that your wrong doings are part of the enemy's plot, you can stand your ground. The idea is that the enemy will have nothing by which he can accuse you of, because you believe your sins were already forgiven during prayer and through the blood-shed of Jesus Christ.

1. **Everything falls into place.**

This is the stage everyone wants to be at. It becomes easy to give up those things that don't contribute to your divine calling. You recognise that some opportunities are seasonal. For example, I left voluntary work as a mentor due to poor health. When I returned to my role as mentor after recovering my health, I did not feel comfortable. I knew that spiritually God had closed those doors and it was time to move on. I got a job around the same time and I enjoyed my new place of work and always saw it as a gift than a burden. Everything else seemed to fall in place, simply because of God's favor.

2. **What you were once afraid of is no longer your fear.**

In pursuit of your purpose, God may have exposed the fear to you so you can identify exactly what it is that was making you afraid. You begin to see yourself bigger than that fear. For example, in public speaking you will need to understand that the people who need to be there will be there because you have something valuable to share and that you are willing to give.

3. **You appreciate the small things.**

You will feel at peace even in the midst of adversity. You will see your challenges as a project to overcome. These challenges don't wear you down, because you know they will soon pass. You understand people and their behaviour, your relationship with everyone is peaceable. The wrong people eventually leave you alone because they see you differently through your actions and bold choices. 'Your team destiny' encourage you and are genuinely happy for you.

4. **You do not procrastinate.**

You stop giving yourself excuses and you get things done. You easily give yourself to prayer. Your prayers are sincere and heart-felt rather than it feeling like a house chore. You sense victory each time you pray or read the word of God.

5. **You understand that your destiny is ongoing.**

You are afraid of making choices. You understand that God orchestrates your steps. You would listen to your instincts if something is not right. Overall you feel excited about life and are ready to embrace the progress.

About the Author

PRISCA IS DEVOTED TO STUDYING God's word and seeing the results that yield holiness and fruitfulness, in this present world. A keen steward and / learner of the word of God, with all diligence, seeks to enlighten her readers and challenge their current situation in their relationship with God.

Prisca has spent over two years volunteering as a peer- mentor and peer-coach at a nonprofit charity organisation, whose aim is to help young people to overcome difficult situations and help them to maximise their potentials and to achieve their dreams and aspirations.

Enjoyed this book?

Please send your review to **authenticauthors@writeme.com**

ENDNOTES

1. 92% of people never follow through on their new year's goals: http://www.goalband.co.uk/goal-achievement-facts.html

2. what destiny? The definition of 'destiny' https://www.quora.com/What-is-the-origin-of-the-word-destiny

3. To meditate means to reflect, ponder, ruminate, revolve constantly. All direct Hebrew dictionary app IW-EN Dictionary v2.1.1

4. an idol can also be… (vocabulary.com) https://www.google.co.uk/search?q=Dictionary#dobs=idol

5. can we be good without God? John Blanchard (2016)

6. *"*Energy cannot be created or destroyed...*~ Albert Einstein Source taken from http://www.goodreads.com/quotes/4455-energy-cannot-be-created-or-destroyed-it- can-only-be

7. Water: www.nestle-waters.com/healthy…/water-functions- in-human-body

8. The Hebrew word is Pistueo, which means to trust,

9. Belief in the Oxford dictionary is a strong feeling that something is true

10. Russian proverb "it is better to vote for what you want…." Source is taken from https://idiomation.wordpress.com/2014/03/14/measure-twice-cut-once/

www.ingramcontent.com/pod-product-compliance
Lightning Source LLC
Chambersburg PA
CBHW050441010526
44118CB00013B/1625